LEONARD INSTRUMENTAL PLAY-ALONG

CLASSICAL SOLOS FOR OBOE

VOLUME 2

The enclosed audio CD is also a CD-ROM and includes:
Piano accompaniment for each solo in PDF format for printing.
Tempo Adjustment Software for use with most PC or Mac computers. Instructions included.

ISBN 978-1-4803-5116-5

HAL•LEONARD® CORPORATION

7777 W. BLUEMOUND RD. P.O. BOX 13819 MILWAUKEE, WI 53213

Visit Hal Leonard Online at
www.halleonard.com

LARGO
from *Xerxes*

GEORGE FRIDERIC HANDEL
Arranged by PHILIP SPARKE

OBOE

00121136

SONGS MY MOTHER TAUGHT ME

3

from *Gypsy Songs*

ANTONÍN DVORÁK
Arranged by PHILIP SPARKE

OBOE

00121136

MINUET NO. 2
from *Notebook for Anna Magdalena Bach*

Attributed to CHRISTIAN PEZOLD
Arranged by PHILIP SPARKE

OBOE

00121136

LA CINQUANTAINE

from *Two Pieces for Cello and Piano*

JEAN GABRIEL-MARIE
Arranged by PHILIP SPARKE

OBOE

00121136

SEE, THE CONQUERING HERO COMES

from *Judas Maccabeus*

GEORGE FRIDERIC HANDEL
Arranged by PHILIP SPARKE

OBOE

SONATINA
Op. 36, No. 1

MUZIO CLEMENTI
Arranged by PHILIP SPARKE

OBOE

Allegro (♩ = 88)

SERENATA
from *String Quartet, Op. 3, No. 5*

FRANZ JOSEPH HAYDN
Arranged by PHILIP SPARKE

OBOE

Andante cantabile (♩ = 96)

TAMBOURIN
from *Second Suite in E Minor*

JEAN-PHILIPPE RAMEAU
Arranged by PHILIP SPARKE

OBOE

00121136

WALTZ
from *Album for the Young*

PYOTR ILYICH TCHAIKOVSKY
Arranged by PHILIP SPARKE

OBOE

00121136

SONATINA
from *Six Pieces, Op. 3*

CARL MARIA VON WEBER
Arranged by PHILIP SPARKE

OBOE

Moderato e con amore
(♩ = 120)

GAVOTTE

from *Paride ed Elena*

CHRISTOPH GLUCK/arr. JOHANNES BRAHMS

Arranged by PHILIP SPARKE

OBOE

Grazioso (♩ = 72)

SONATA
Op. 118, No. 1

ROBERT SCHUMANN
Arranged by PHILIP SPARKE

OBOE

Moderato
($\quad$ = 104)

00121136

SERENADE
from *Schwanengesang, D.957*

FRANZ SCHUBERT
Arranged by PHILIP SPARKE

OBOE

Andante con moto
(♩ = 84)

SONATINA
Anh. 5, No. 1

LUDWIG VAN BEETHOVEN
Arranged by PHILIP SPARKE

OBOE

Moderato
(♩ = 126)

00121136

BOURRÉE
from *Flute Sonata, HWV 363b*

GEORGE FRIDERIC HANDEL
Arranged by PHILIP SPARKE

OBOE